Don't Be a Chicken... Reach for the Stars

A Practical Handbook to Growing Your Company...and Life at the Same Time

Douglas R. Palmer, CPA

Copyright © 2014 Douglas R. Palmer, CPA

All rights reserved.

ISBN-10: 149539266X
ISBN-13: 978-1495392665

DEDICATION

To dear friends and family who have struggled through life
and passed away without the chance to truly
<u>Reach for the Stars</u>!

CONTENTS

Acknowledgments

Preface — Pg #1

Introduction: "You Can Do Both" — Pg #3

Step 1: Reaching — Pg #6

Step 2: Finances — Pg #15

Step 3: Share the Wealth — Pg #25

Step 4: The Fast Track — Pg #32

Step 5: Support Growth — Pg #41

Step 6: Create Accountability — Pg #51

Step 7: Spreading the Word — Pg #57

Conclusion — Pg #64

ACKNOWLEDGMENTS

I am deeply thankful to the team of people who helped bring this second book together. First and foremost, I would like to thank Lori Wark, who helped me with organizing, rewording, streamlining, and completing this project. Next, I am grateful to numerous theological teachings and prayer life, as well as to friends and colleagues who have mentored me through the years and helped me to arrive at the conclusion that one can grow a large business and life at the same time.

PREFACE

If you've read my first book in the Don't Be a Chicken series, *A Practical Handbook to Starting a Successful Business*, you already know that a deadly infection in my finger sustained from a broken light bulb changed the course of my life. Miraculously, after an operation and high doses of antibiotics, I pulled through. Given the odds, I was extremely lucky to be alive.

My near-death experience forced me to face the reality of a finite life-span. I knew from that moment I needed to fulfill my dream. I had already created one business, but my aspirations to start other entrepreneurial companies and ventures had been put on the back burner before my run-in with a light bulb. But I worried that the time and energy needed to begin and grow a business would leave little time for the most important part of my life: my family. Over time, I learned how to have a flourishing business without neglecting my family. My motivation for writing this book is to share my knowledge with the fledging entrepreneur who wants to know how to take his or her business to the next level and at the same time have a rich and fulfilling life with time to pursue other interests and passions.

As in my previous book, at the beginning of each chapter I've listed key points that are discussed in the related chapter. At the end of each chapter, I list questions to help you understand how the information you've just read should be applied to your particular business. Take time to consider your answers. You may even want to write down your thoughts and ideas. A written record of your learning process is a great road map toward making your business and the life you want more than just an idea.

INTRODUCTION: "YOU CAN DO BOTH"

The challenge of the work-life balance is without question one of the most significant struggles faced by modern man.
—Stephen Covey (RIP)

THREE KEYS
1. Grow your business and keep your life.
2. Don't shy away from work or family life—embrace both.
3. Focus efforts on values.

Scott didn't mince words. He said what he thought, especially if he was trying to save a company or help a friend. I met him through one of my clients, where he was doing just that—laying it on the line to my client about what needed to be done to keep the business solvent. When I met Scott he was a seasoned business owner in his fifties, a bearded hard charger who smoked and eventually took up riding a motorcycle. He became my friend.

A few years later, Scott came to a crossroads and needed to wind down his business. He suggested I buy his company, but I too was at a crossroads. I wanted to try my hand at creating new companies, and I longed to take on the challenges necessary to fulfill my dreams, but I worried such an endeavor would steal precious time away from my family. In a series of e-mails, Scott and I debated the issue. I confided my biggest concern by writing: "I battle with this inside. I'm torn between wanting to be a successful/rich businessman and a good father. I ask myself, can I do both? I haven't found the answer yet."

Scott wrote back with an answer that has always stayed with me: "Let me say this regarding your one great concern in life, that of being forced to decide whether to be a rich, successful businessman or to be a great father. In my humble opinion, you can have both. In fact, it is in the very act of striving to do both that you will find the clearest path leading to both."

My friend was right. It hasn't always been easy, but the act of striving to find the balance has shown me the "clearest path" to having a successful business and a great life. It *is* possible to have both.

Scott always believed in sharing his experiences and wisdom to help others. In honor of his spirit of generosity, I have written this book in the hope that sharing the knowledge and experience I have gained over the years will help you build a successful, thriving business without leaving your life behind.

STEP 1: REACHING

The brave man is not he who does not feel afraid, but he who conquers that fear.
—Nelson Mandela (RIP)

THREE KEYS
1. Find your values and write them down.
2. Turn written values into a balance wheel.
3. Don't shy away from reaching—ATTACK.

Is it time?

                  Grow Your Business…

You've been in business for a number of years, nurturing your company as you transform it from an idea to a reality. The business is doing fine, and you're enjoying the fruits of your hard work. Is this the time to begin to move your company to the next level? Is the next level even something you want? You're the only one who can answer these questions. There are no benchmarks or watershed moments that shout "it's time to grow." The decision must be based on your personal and business goals and your gut instinct.

Yes, growing your business will seem overwhelming—and at times it will be—but if you follow a few simple steps, reaching for that brass ring will be a lot easier.

So if your head, heart, and the pit of your stomach are sending you messages, check out the following section, which lays out the steps to answer that call.

Identify Core Values

What kind of business do you want? Do you have some personal core values that you want reflected in your company? It's important to honestly answer these questions so you can build a business you can be proud of and one that makes a statement about who you are and your core values. Write down the core business values and review periodically. Revise as your business expands or changes.

Mission Statement

With this twenty- to thirty-word statement you get to tell *why* you are pursing your vision. What's your reason for starting this particular business, and what special talents or experiences do you possess that will make your vision a reality? Write your answers down and review and revise regularly.

ATTACK

A. *Accept the Mission*

Don't shy away from the mission. Aggressively pursue the mission.

T. *Trust Yourself*

Be confident and trust your instincts.

T. *Trust Others*

Leverage when growing a company is very important. The key in growth is to find great people and trust them.

A. *Assign Tasks*

Clearly identify the tasks of the mission and assign the tasks to each key person.

C. *Create Milestones*

Break the mission into smaller milestones. Apply the old adage "the best way to eat an elephant is one bite at a time" to your mission.

K. *Keep Balance Always*

Keep overall balance and perspective in mind and remember to have fun!

Handbook Questions (for Your Company):

- Have you written down the core values for your growing business?
- How have these values changed from the time when the business was a start-up?
- Have you written down *why* you are pursuing this vision?
- Have you *attacked* your mission lately?

Grow Your Life...

Life can grow in all areas...

The methods for growing your life are surprisingly similar to how you grow your business. Management, care, and forethought are already part of your business plan, and they should also become a part of your life plan.

Identify Core Values

Just as in business, your first step to reaching goals in your life is to identify what kind of life, outside of business, you want to create. Ask yourself, what are your goals and passions? Write your answers down and review or revise periodically. This will help you remember what makes your life complete, especially when you start to feel you can't possibly squeeze any more into your day.

Mission Statement

The next step is to steal skills you have learned from the business world and use them as tools for growing your life. Just as a mission statement is essential to a business, a life mission statement, or life values list, is essential to your life. This short statement documents your passions and is a written testament to what you want to accomplish separate from your business.

Write your life mission statement down and include specifics—what you want to accomplish, what's most important to you, what makes your heart pound with excitement. Review and revise your mission statement periodically.

Here is my mission statement as an example: "All the while putting God time and family time first, and being ever committed to personal fitness/nutrition, spiritual and mental growth, become financially secure within the next decade so that in the period thereafter I can focus on serving a higher need and performing many more works of charity (including starting a 501c3 charitable organization)."

Balance Wheel

Create a balance wheel to visually represent the core values of your life. This simple image can lead you to understand more about who you are, what your values are, how you are spending your life now, and what you may want to change.

Here is my balance wheel:

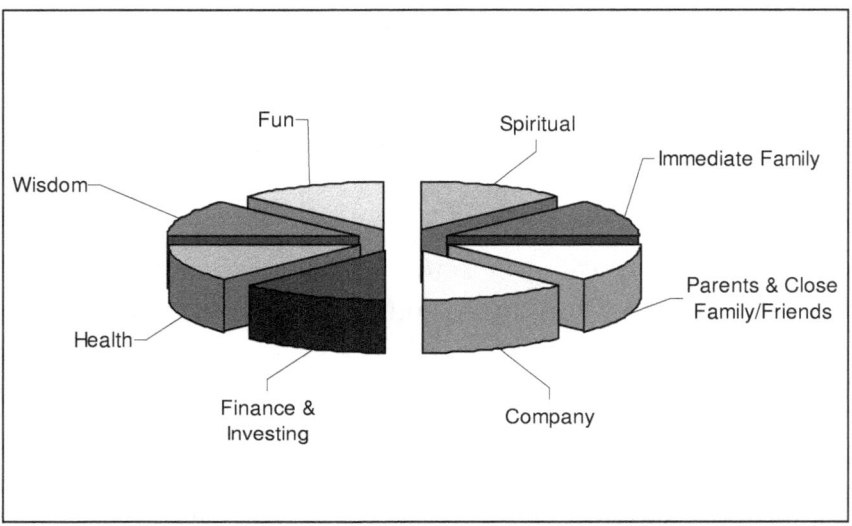

I work hard to keep each segment of my balance wheel equal. When you first create a visual representation of how your life is organized, your balance wheel may not be as equally divided. That's fine if some areas of your life require more focus and you are comfortable with that arrangement. Or you may decide that your life needs to be more balanced. You can work toward your ideal over the weeks ahead.

Weekly Reviews

The key to growing your life is to do weekly reviews. I learned this trick years ago from a book written by James Ball and Jennifer Kuchta called *It's about Time*. In their book, they stress the importance of scheduling weekly meetings (preferably at the end of the week for the next week).

Just as in business, it's important to review your life plans regularly. Without a regular checkup, things can slip through the cracks.

Put on your calendar a weekly meeting with yourself to review your list of values and priorities for your life. Write down a few steps you plan to do during the upcoming week to bring you closer to your goals.

Continue reviewing, assigning tasks, and revising each week. If some tasks are not complete or remain untouched, write down the reasons why. This will help you evaluate what may be getting in the way of growing your life.

Here is an example of a life values list (which mirrors the balance wheel) and action items for the week for each value:

Spiritual	Immediate Family	Parents & Close Family/Friends
• Get out in nature • Go to church • Give to a homeless person	• Date night with wife • Snowboard with daughter • Soccer sign up for son	• Movie with Dad • Lunch with sister • Invite close friend to basketball game
Company	Finance & Investing	Health
• Focus on BD • Update marketing materials	• SEP contribution • Look at stock portfolio • Update budget	• Run three times per week • Get cholesterol checked • Play tennis

	Fun
Wisdom • Listen to MorningCoach.com • Find mastermind group • Prepare speech for toastmasters • Buy recommended book and read a chapter	**Fun** • Go to movie • Schedule trip for summer

You will see that the above tasks each address one of my eight important values. These tasks can also be performed in a week's time. They are not necessarily goals or bucket-list items.

Handbook Questions (for Your Life):

- Have you created a life mission statement?
- Have you written down your core values (your balance wheel)?
- Have you created a list of a few action items to address each one of these core values?
- Have you scheduled a weekly meeting with yourself to create a list for the following week?

STEP 2: FINANCES

Every step in life shows much caution is required.
—Johann Wolfgang von Goethe

THREE KEYS
1. While growing your company, keep expenses intact and profits in line.
2. Hold weekly meetings with yourself.
3. Revisit long-term goals and set weekly goals each week.

Grow Your Business...

T he basics.

Let's start with the basics. If your processes for managing the in-and-out-flow of money are nonexistent, it's time to rethink how to manage your money.

• *Stay on top of collections.* Aggressively follow up on all outstanding invoices. Unpaid invoices create instability and lead to cash flow problems.
• *Collect up front.* Make sure that all of your contracts stipulate payment upfront. Net thirty can stretch into net sixty.
• *Turn unused equipment into cash.* Don't let any equipment sit around. If it's not being used, sell it.
• *Limit company credit cards.* Only when necessary, provide your executives with corporate credit cards. Don't give credit cards to your entire staff.
• *Manage accounts payable.* Keep as much cash as possible in the bank at all times. To do this, pay only critical vendors first. Then pace vendor payments in relation to receivable collections. Stay away from automatic payments on credit cards. Instead, have invoices sent to you even for recurring items so you can verify charges.

The Pursuit of Payment

If you're not getting paid for work accomplished, your business will not grow and may even crumble. Without a doubt, one of the biggest challenges that small businesses face is being paid on time. Getting clients to pay on time is an art form that takes a certain amount of finesse, tenacity, and relationship building. The following is a quick tutorial on the art of getting paid.

• Have your finance person or accounting department follow up on all payment matters. If you are the person doing work for a client or customer, it helps if you are not the one following up on payment-related matters. If you do not have someone to make collections, find someone.

• Send invoices out in advance. If the work is going to be performed and billed on a certain completion date, send the invoice out in advance of that date with the expected completion date on the invoice. The goal is to get the invoice into your accounting system and in the hands of the client as quickly as possible.

• Send regular statements. Set up a system to send out invoices on a monthly basis at a minimum (via e-mail and a hard copy).

• Stay on top of outstanding payments. Periodically review your accounts receivable report and create a process of sending statements to clients who are delinquent.

• Befriend your client's accounts payable person. The old adage "you get more flies with honey" is true even when trying to get paid for work performed. Make every correspondence with your client's accounting department upbeat and friendly and always send thank-you e-mails for help in sorting out payment issues.

- Talk to others in the client's organization. If the accounting person seems to be ignoring your appeals, chances are there is a reason. Those working in accounts payable are usually agnostic with respect to who is getting paid, so talk to your customer liaison as soon as possible to find out why the bills are not being paid.
- Stay away from lawsuits. In my early years of business ownership, I was keen to involve a collection lawyer early in the process. I have found that it is much easier to appeal to a person's sense of doing the right thing than to threaten a lawsuit. If you are dealing with a client who is not responding to your queries, however, having a lawyer write a letter may be your only recourse.

Maintain Your Profit and Loss (P and L)

For any small business, managing revenues, costs, and expenses comes with inherent challenges. I have developed the following tips to help small businesses maintain their P and Ls.

Revenue
- Create a revenue plan and hold employees accountable for sticking to that plan.
- Lock down customers with long-term contracts if possible.
- "Love" your existing customers and keep them happy. Send thank-you cards or buy them an occasional thank-you present.
- Grow revenue with existing customers by finding ways to expand services.
- Get rid of undesirable clients.

• Use a sales tracking software that manages contacts and sales activities to help you keep focused on new client opportunities.

• Have an action plan for growth and action.

• Plan for downturns by maintaining reserve funds so you won't be caught off guard.

Expenses

• Revisit P and L results on a monthly basis. Include spending on assets and depreciation (a non–P and L item) in the monthly review. This is an area where spending can get out of hand and often gets overlooked.

• Ensure expenses can easily be identified and categorized.

• Continually compare results against income and expense benchmarks.

• Make sure employee costs, such as salary, benefits and overhead, are not more than 50 percent of revenue.

• Verify that rent is no more than 3 to 6 percent of company revenue and 5 to 10 percent of revenue is devoted to business development.

• Incentivize appropriate employees around expense goals to ensure the company stays lean.

• Ensure that the company is profitable and keeps a healthy margin as a buffer for downturns.

• Keep and maintain projections that include actual results *plus* forward-looking projections for the year.

• Perform a vendor analysis annually to validate that vendor expenses are not widely out of whack.

Your Banker

In my first book, *A Practical Handbook: Starting a Successful Business*, I stressed the importance of establishing a relationship with a banker, someone who understands small businesses and is willing to work closely with you. As your company grows, this relationship becomes even more important.

Personal Guarantee

In my first book I advised business owners to establish a line of credit with their bankers to cover large outlays or working capital needs. If you have done so, the line of credit you established probably required a personal guarantee, which meant if you ran into financial difficulty, the bank had the right to make claims against your company and your personal assets. If your business is a company with partners or if you expect to take on partners in the future, a personal guarantee could create unnecessary paperwork, as partners will need to submit personal financial statements each year the line of credit is renewed or if the amount increases.

Now that you have an established, profit-making business, ask your banker to remove the personal guarantee, and if he or she won't, find a bank that will accommodate your request. A business with a track record of profitability and financial responsibility is a good catch for a financial institution, so many banks will be willing to compete for your business.

Debt Is Good

Taking on debt may seem counterintuitive, but there are instances when a little debt goes a long way to growing a business.

Five reasons for taking on debt are:

• Debt can be cheap. The Small Business Administration (SBA) offers loans, which can be inexpensive relative to equity financing (due to shareholder dilution). This means that there exists a potential to benefit greatly from the gains due to the leverage.

• There are tax benefits. Interest on debt is tax deductible, whereas dividends on equity are not deductible (and actually can be taxable). In fact, the higher the marginal tax rate of the company, the higher the amount of debt a company should have in its tax structure.

• Debt provides an incentive for efficiency. Debt adds an element of discipline to an organization. The old adage "equity is a cushion; debt is a sword" certainly applies. In fact, the management teams of firms with high cash flows left over each year are more likely to be complacent and inefficient.

• Ownership stays the same. Financing through debt keeps the control of an organization intact.

While taking on debt can push your business to the next level, there are some pitfalls, such as:

- Debt holders have a lien on your company.
- Debt payment amounts can be onerous.
- Interest rates can be too high (depending on the circumstances). Debt can come with an equity piece that dilutes the company.

One of the biggest downsides to debt is the possibility of

being forced into bankruptcy or being taken over by a lending institution. Although this is a possibility, generally banks have little interest in acquiring a company that has fallen behind in payments or has broken a financial covenant. Banks would much rather work with a company than take it over.

Handbook Questions (for Your Company):

- Have you written down your collections and money management processes?
- Have you documented the controls in place for your business? For each significant risk area, what controls have you established?
- Have you looked closely at your P and L and balance sheet? What customers can you "lock down" for a longer time period? What expenses have crept up that you can cut?

Grow Your Life...

The principles of managing money for a business or your life are pretty much the same. There's no need to reinvent the wheel here. In order to maintain control over your life finances, you need to create a budget and always maintain a reserve account for those unexpected emergencies. Unlike your business financial strategy, however, your personal plan should stay clear of debt.

It's a good idea to review your personal finances weekly. Put this review on your calendar. Perhaps the financial review could coincide with your weekly life mission statement evaluation.

Create a Budget

Create a personal budget and stick to it.

- Use a simple spreadsheet (don't make it complicated).
- In the first column include all bank accounts and total liquid investments.
- In the same column below the cash balances have a row for each recurring expense and bills (mortgage, electricity, etc.).
- Below that, in the same row, have amounts for inflows

of money (earnings, rental income).
- Summarize and arrive at a net spending or saving amount.
- Keep goals on the spreadsheet.
- Update this regularly.
- Keep a sense of control and stay organized.

For some great tips for creating a simple budget, please visit J. B. Glossinger's tips on YouTube: http://www.youtube.com/watch?v=ZDRx5SjUwt4.

The key to a solid financial life is to remember that life should be simple and filled with nonmonetary rewards.

Handbook Questions (for Your Life):

- Have you identified unnecessary debt in your life and developed a plan to eliminate it?
- Have you created a personal budget?
- Have you revisited your finances this week?

STEP 3: SHARE THE WEALTH

If you're in the luckiest 1 percent of humanity, you owe it to the rest of humanity to think about the other 99 percent.
—Warren Buffet

FOUR KEYS
1. Reward employees with equity.
2. Find partners.
3. Outsource all parts of your life.
4. Give back.

Grow Your Business...

Now that you are a pro at guarding your assets, I am now going to do what may appear to be a complete reversal and recommend spending money in ways that may not seem directly beneficial to the bottom line. However, there are times when you need to think beyond the boundaries of your balance sheet.

Finance Your Dream

A Practical Handbook to Starting a Successful Business went into significant detail about financing a start-up company with the help of family, friends, and angel investors. Although they offer a great way to get your company off the ground by providing seed money, these sources tend to fund at fairly low levels. Companies wanting to grow exponentially need to find a large source of financing. Teaming up with a venture capitalist or a deep-pocketed investor may be the way to go.

Your first thought may be: "Wait a minute. If I take on an investor that means my share of the company is diminished. I just lost a piece of the pie." That may be true in the short term, but only with a significant influx of cash can your company grow and in the process gain more equity, which is your ultimate goal.

Reward Your Employees

Unless you are able to hire and keep highly qualified and experienced employees, your company is doomed to stagnation. One way to attract and keep talented people on board is to offer employee stock options.

Again, employee stock options may sound like another way to "dilute" your equity in the company. However, stock option benefits tend to attract and keep talented employees who are dedicated to the company. After all, they have a stake in the company's success.

Find Partners

To grow, you need partners, plain and simple. Partners bring a range of skills and talents to the table that might be missing from your business. A partner with different expertise and life experiences generates new ideas and visions. You've been alone in the trenches for a while and may have tunnel vision at this point. With the right partner, your business can grow in ways that were not even on your radar screen.

So, who's the "right partner"? Think of a partnership like a marriage. You're going to be spending a lot of time with this person. You're going to be making some pretty important decisions with this person, and there are going to be good days and bad days—times when you and your partner will be in sync and other moments when visions may conflict. Are you starting to get the marriage analogy?

A partner should be someone with whom you feel you can develop a good working relationship—someone you trust who will have the best interests of the company as a priority. The right partner is someone you can hash out conflicts and differences of opinion within a healthy debate.

It may be tempting to take on a family member or a close friend as a partner. A word of warning: a personal relationship frequently comes with some extra baggage. Unless these issues can be sorted out or kept completely separate from the business, you could lose a friend or end up with an angry family member.

If you don't have a personal relationship with the partner you are considering, do your homework. Conduct a background check, take a look at the person's financial situation, and discuss his or her goals and expectations. Look for a partner who complements your skills and talents and avoid someone who has the exact same skill set as you. This type of person won't bring anything extra to the company, and a duplication of skills may initiate conflict over responsibilities. You could also close the door to new ideas and new perspectives by partnering with a clone of yourself.

When a partner is brought on board, start the relationship on the road to success from the start. Map out the responsibilities for yourself and the partner. This helps establish the division of labor and minimizes conflicts. Partners should also be put in charge of specific divisions and be accountable for the profit and loss of those areas of responsibility. Specify the rules about spending and when sign-off by both partners is required.

Purchase a life insurance policy on each of your partners and insert a disability clause. If the unexpected happens, your business can still continue, either through death benefit funds or a buyout in the event of a disability.

Handbook Questions (for Your Company):

- Have you explored financing business growth through raising equity?
- Have you created a stock option pool for employees?
- Have you looked for a partner?
- Have you performed your due diligence on your potential partner?

Grow Your Life...

By now you must be thinking, "Yeah, this is all well and good, but running a business is taking up every spare minute of my day. How do I carve out time for my life?"

Outsource

There are many time-wasting actions that we perform each day that do not correlate to our list of values.

Carving out time for your life is similar to streamlining and creating an efficient business. To get everything you need done, you hire or outsource to specialists in their fields. The same strategy applies to your life.

Write down all of the time-wasting activities that do not add to your weekly values. Then find and hire people who can help with tasks that you don't have the skills or time to do. Hire a person to help with the housework. Look for a company that specializes in helping with errands or shopping. If you have a garden, and gardening is not one of your life passions, find a gardener. These tasks can suck up a lot of time—time you could be spending doing things with your family, following your interests, or going after your life goals.

Develop a good relationship with a child-care provider. This person can take care of some of the everyday tasks of child care, leaving you the opportunity for lots of quality time with your children.

For great ideas on how to outsource parts of life, read *The 4-Hour Workweek* by Tim Ferriss.

Give Back

Your business is growing, and your income is growing. Through hard work and risk taking, you've been very fortunate. Don't forget to say thanks to the universe for your fortune by giving back.

It has been my experience that life is a cycle of giving and receiving from the universe. The more one gives, the more one receives in return. It took me a long time to understand this principle. However, when I finally became enlightened, I realized this to be true. The more I gave to charity, the more my businesses seemed to thrive—and I felt better.

Donate to charities that mean something to you; give to the eleemosynary institutions of your choice. If you feel the need to make your giving more personal, find organizations in your neighborhood that could use a helping hand.

Handbook Questions (for Life):

- Have you outsourced the parts of your life that take lots of time but do not add to your values wheel?
- Have you written down these time-wasting activities and effectively found someone to perform these tasks? Have you read *The 4-Hour Workweek* by Tim Ferriss?
- Have you given back to the universe lately?

STEP 4: THE FAST TRACK

Unless you are running scared all the time, you're gone.
—Bill Gates

> THREE KEYS
> 1. Expand your company through buying a business.
> 2. Create a bucket list.
> 3. Have stretch goals.

Grow Your Business...

While a great product or service, advertising, word of mouth, and the ability to meet customers' needs will increase your business over time, some steps can be taken to kick your company to the next level faster than through traditional business practices.

Buy a Business

The purchase of a successful, ready-made business in the same or complementary line of work can immediately get you in league with the big boys. But how do you go about finding and buying a business? Here are some methods.

Business Brokers

Business brokers assist small companies in buying and selling businesses. The job of a business broker is to estimate the values of businesses, search for appropriate buyers or sellers, set up interviews between the parties, and help with negotiations. Most business brokers are commission based with the seller paying the fees. Fees range from 5 to 10 percent of the sale price of the company. To find a business broker, search the Internet and ask companies in your industry for recommendations.

Investment Banker

Business brokers are usually small companies, while investment brokers are larger and employ a large staff with a wide variety of skills and knowledge. Investment bankers are more expensive than business brokers, but if you feel that you've outgrown a business broker, an investment banker may be the next step. Frequently sellers looking for buyers hire investment bankers, but these companies will also work with buyers to scout out potential companies in a similar industry.

An investment banker can also help you with roll-up transactions, which can grow your company quickly. A roll-up describes the acquisition of several small companies offering the same or similar products or services. The companies are frequently merged, which reduces costs due to economies of scale.

Although it is a great way to ramp up your company, bringing several businesses under one brand can be challenging. Different cultures and business practices have been known to thwart efforts to create a cohesive entity.

Whether you are looking for a single purchase or a roll-up, make sure you are hiring the right investment banker for your company. Your chosen candidate should:

- Know your industry inside and out.
- Have a database of companies to call on your behalf.
- Have access to capital you may need.

The agreement between you and an investment banker is usually in the form of an engagement letter. Here are some items to check before you sign off.

- *Term.* The agreement should stipulate a commitment of no more than six to twelve months.
- *Flexibility.* If the relationship is not working, the agreement should allow you to terminate at any

point.
- *Payment.* Compensation should be on a transactional basis, meaning the investment banker only gets paid once a transaction is finalized.

Retirement Sale

Another good way to find a company is to connect with a business owner who is about to retire. Finding such a business can be as easy as approaching an owner and inquiring if he or she would like to sell.

Retiring business owners usually have worked a long time in developing their companies, and your assurance that under your guidance their customers will be well taken care of may be just what they need to consider the deal. As an added incentive, you might offer your services on a temporary basis so the owner can get to know you while you learn the business under his or her tutelage.

As you discuss the potential buy, listen to the business owner to understand what his or her needs are, and try to address any concerns. The two of you may come up with some inventive ways to work out a deal that meets both your needs. Often the decision to sell or not to sell is less financial and more a desire to sell to the right person. It's important to keep in mind this is a person's life work and that person wants to make sure that his or her company is passed on to a good steward.

Just Ask

The simple act of asking can open many doors once you find a business in which you are interested. You'll be surprised how many people are looking to sell. To find potential companies:

- Participate in functions or join organizations associated with your target companies.
- Get involved in the chamber of commerce.
- Go to networking events.
- Research your competitors who might be in the market to sell.

Finding the Right Rainmaker

To grow organically, hire an experienced rainmaker—someone who has a proven track record of bringing in business.

Rainmakers are out there, but just as in the Katherine Hepburn movie *The Rainmaker*, not all are what they say they are. To find the rainmaker who is right for your business, verify the potential candidate actually has brought in substantial business at other companies. Make sure the rainmaker understands your company and what types of clients or businesses are best. You may want to give this person a personality test, which can quickly uncover whether the two of you will mesh.

A talented, well-connected rainmaker can make a big difference in the bottom line of a company, so do your homework. A wrong choice may not be discovered for months or even years down the road, costing you lots of unrealized revenue.

Helping the Rainmaker Make Rain

Make sure the rainmaker is aligned with your goals and your vision. Share your thoughts on how you want to grow the company so you are both pointing in the same direction. Any differences of opinion could cost your company millions of dollars.

Have your rainmaker review your five-year projection plan and verify he or she is on board with all your assumptions for growth. If your rainmaker believes the goal of the company is to grow at a 10 percent clip per year and you're planning a 50 percent growth rate, there are going to be significant problems.

This may sound backward, but the rainmaker should be compensated at a higher rate than you, the business owner. You are depending on this person to bring in a specified amount of business. The incentive to "hit the numbers" must be significant.

The rainmaker also needs some room to spread his or her wings within the structure and goals of your business. Allow your rainmaker to hire his or her team and encourage innovation in selling your product.

Handbook Questions (for Your Company):

- Have you looked into purchasing a business? Have you contacted either a business broker or an investment banker?
- Have you studied the market, networked, and found an opportunity to purchase a company?
- Have you explored other businesses with retirement-aged owners?
- Have you searched for a key sales person?

Grow Your Life...

You've been thinking about a number of passion projects for a long time. Somehow you keep shifting these life goals to the "it would be nice list" with the excuse that you're too busy building a business. At some point you might ask yourself, if now isn't the time, when is? Of course, you are busy, so you need to make an actionable plan to accomplish those projects that keep pulling at your heartstrings.

The Bucket List

The bucket list has become somewhat of a cliché, but the concept is valid. Call it a bucket list, a passion project list, my life goals, or whatever resonates with you, the idea is the same. Write down your life goals with the steps needed to achieve each item and make a plan to act. List even those goals that may be a long shot, but are achievable.

I discovered the power of the bucket list via reading a book written by Ted Leonsis, a billionaire technology executive and owner of a few professional sports teams. In his book, *The Business of Happiness,* he tells his story of being in a plane that almost crashed when he was a young man. Although he had recently sold his first company and had a lot of money, he had not experienced a lot of what life had to offer.

As a result of this near-death experience, Ted created a bucket list. Some of the items on this list were materialistic and others stretched goals and dreams. The amazing thing about this bucket list was that he has "crossed off" a number of items on this list so far—including owning a sports team.

Your bucket list should include all aspects of your life and cover everything you want to experience in life. Here are a few items from my bucket list (some already checked off):

- Start a charity.
- Do mission work in Africa.
- Buy a retirement home in Florida.
- Take a Galapagos dive trip.
- Bike ride through Europe.
- Write a book.
- Complete an executive education program.

Review your bucket list regularly—at least weekly—and tick off the steps to final accomplishment. You may not reach every single goal exactly as you had imagined, but your list will remind you that there is no time like the present.

Handbook Questions (for Life):

- Have you created your bucket list?
- Does your list include all facets of what you want out of life?
- Do you regularly refer to this list during your weekly meetings?

Step 5: SUPPORT GROWTH

My favorite things in life don't cost any money. It's really clear that the most precious resource we all have is time.
—Steve Jobs

THREE KEYS
1. Grow your sales team.
2. Hire a coach.
3. Create boundaries between your work & personal life.

Grow Your Business...

A growing business needs a structure that can support growth. As your workforce grows, distribution expands, and processes become more complex, a plan must be in place to accommodate the changes that come with growth. Begin the expansion of your business with the following actions in mind.

Grow Your Sales Team

A creative, talented, and assertive sales team is critical to any business. In fact, the best salespeople frequently get paid even more than the founders of the company because the sales staff is bringing in customers and growing the revenue.

I would recommend getting help in hiring the sales staff, whether through a recruiting agency or an experienced human resource professional. Remember, if you hire the wrong person for the job, you may not feel the effects of this bad decision for many months.

I would also recommend requiring prospective employees to take a series of tests. Look for companies that help businesses hire people using aptitude tests specifically geared to evaluating those looking for jobs in sales. A good company to hire for employee measurement tools and screening tests is PSP METRICS (http://www.pspmetrics.com/).

Don't pass up the opportunity to check references to make sure candidates were really as successful at their former jobs as their résumés make you believe.

Make Sales People Accountable

My number one rule of growing a sales team is to develop a plan that outlines your expectations.

Sales people are notorious for hitting their numbers early in the quarter and then coasting the rest of the quarter, backdating or forward dating to disguise their tactics. Therefore, management should set up systems of daily accountability for the people who sell the company's products.

Find Channel Partners

The term *channel partners* refers to a relationship where a company partners with another company to market or sell their products or services. If you create a channel partner, your products can reach a wider audience with less time and effort.

For the most part, you'll know the companies in your industry that are appropriate channel partners. However, to broaden your pool of channel choices, search the Internet and talk to people you know who may have suggestions.

Before you make an agreement with any channel partners, verify that potential candidates have effective teams in place and are technically proficient to showcase your products.

The secret to creating a good channel-partner relationship is an agreement that specifies the terms and how much you will pay your partners, generally through commissions.

When coming up with a fee structure, keep in mind that you want to create an incentive for your partners to push your product versus another product. In today's market, it's getting harder to cut through the clutter. Channel partners are one way to get your products or services before a wider audience so the money spent is well worth it.

Outsource Human Resources

When companies go through a phase of needing to hire a lot of employees quickly, as in the case of growing a business, owners are frequently caught off guard. Companies may lack an adequate human resource department or may not have processes in place for a large influx of employees. To get around these potential stumbling blocks and to ensure that all aspects of hiring new employees move ahead smoothly, consider outsourcing the human resource function. There are many talented recruiting firms all over the country that focus on hiring the best employees for an organization.

The need to hire a large number of people is cyclical. When the crunch is over, you may need only a few HR staff to handle employee benefits, personnel issues, etc., which can be performed by the in-house staff.

Create Systems

As discussed in detail in my first book, *A Practical Handbook to Starting a Business*, the key to growing an organization is developing a framework of solid, efficient systems and processes for all business-related tasks, such as accounting, human resources, delivery of products, and billing clients. These systems should be documented and distributed to everyone in the company. While this is important for just about any company in any stage of development, if you want to expand and grow, creating and documenting processes becomes especially critical. With a larger staff, more clients or products, more divisions, and more complexity, you need to find ways your business can run itself, while still generating income and minimizing downtime. With well-documented processes, if an employee leaves, someone can step in and perform the tasks without a steep learning curve. If someone on the team is suddenly unavailable for an extended period of time, even if this person is a key employee, another person can easily step in.

Documenting day-to-day processes may seem arduous and time consuming, but the time spent not only creates efficiency, but also gives you a greater understanding of what's involved in running your business. It may also shed some light on ways to streamline.

Ensure Employee Benefits Are Sustainable

As you bring more employees on board, make sure that the benefits you offered when there were fewer employees can scale up to accommodate a larger staff. A company that offers overly generous benefits when it only has a few employees may find it hard to maintain the same benefits as it grows. Downsizing benefits can create problems for those employees who see their benefits decrease from the "good old days."

Handbook Questions (for Your Company):

- Do you have a sales structure in place? Have you hired a sales team?
- Are the sales people made accountable?
- Have you found channel partners for your product or service?
- Do you have a recruiter in place to hire your team?
- Have you documented your critical business systems? Have you hired someone to document your controls?
- Have you hired a consultant to look at your company benefits?

Grow Your Life...

It's amazing how quickly running a business can infiltrate every corner of your life without your being aware it's happening. You may at this point feel it's become impossible to pry your business from your life. Take heart—there are a few simple steps you can take to create a definitive boundary between your business and your life.

Growing your life in this instance starts with taking control of your business. Setting up processes and systems will help control the overflow into your life.

Manage Your E-mail

If you're the type of person who is controlled by e-mail, setting up a system for managing your e-mail for your business will control the frenzy when you're "off duty." Make it a habit to check your e-mail only twice a day. Turn off e-mail notifications. That ping can get you salivating like Pavlov's dog to check on the latest message.

If you need a little motivation to get off the e-mail merry-go-round, a recent study by University of California at Irvine and the US Army that found a stress link to e-mail may be just what you need. Using heart rate monitors, researchers found that people who continually checked e-mail were in a "high alert" state and they tended to multitask more, a topic I'll get to shortly. When subjects were away from their e-mail for five days, their heart rates went back to normal and they were able to focus more.[1]

E-mail checking is a hard addiction to overcome, but just this one step will make you more efficient, cut down on stress, and leave time for your life.

Go Paperless

Even in your personal life going paperless is a good idea. The less paper the less clutter which can be a time waster when you need to figure out what to do with all that stuff. Making everything electronic and setting up a good file structure on your computer is quicker and easier than dealing with paper. Plus you always know where everything is—no time is lost searching for that one critical piece of paper in a pile of other pieces of paper. Use Dropbox to transfer documents electronically and Evernote to keep notes to yourself. You may even want to keep your bucket list in Evernote. That way you can save URLs or items of interest regarding your life goals all in one place.

Don't Multitask

It is pure fiction that humans can multitask. The brain is just not wired to perform two tasks at the same time. When you think you're multitasking what you're really doing is

---

[1] "Email 'Vacations' Decrease Stress, Increase Concentration, *UCIrvine Today*, May 3, 2012, http://today.uci.edu/news/2012/05/nr_email_120503.php.

switch tasking, moving back and forth between tasks. Switch tasking is a time waster. Time spent going back and forth between tasks adds up. Another study by University of California at Irvine, as reported by *The New Atlantis*, found that workers who multitasked or switch tasked wasted on average 25 minutes.[2] Timothy Ferriss, best-selling author of the book *The 4-Hour Workweek*, is unequivocal in his advice about multitasking: Don't do it. As he writes, "Divided attention will result in more frequent interruptions, lapses in concentration, poorer net results, and less gratification."[3]

So in business and in life, stop multitasking or switch tasking. Instead set aside blocks of time of at least an hour per task. The focus you spend without switching to another task will in the long run help you to get more done and with greater accuracy and efficiency. When you're working on life goals you need the luxury of time to be able to imagine, dream, and plan.

Hire a Coach

A coach is not just for business. Find a life coach who can be a sounding board for your hopes and dreams. A coach can help keep you inspired and work with you on the steps you need to take to reach your life goals. If you aren't able to find the right coach immediately or you need a little

---

[2] Christine Rosen, "The Myth of Multitasking," *The New Atlantis*, Spring 2008, http://www.thenewatlantis.com/publications/the-myth-of-multitasking.

[3] Timothy Ferriss, *The 4-Hour Workweek*, exp. upd. ed. (New York: Crown, 2009), 83.

extra push, sign up for the morningcoach.com. J. B. Glossinger, the founder of Morning Coach, is inspiring and has great tips.

Handbook Questions (for Life):

- Do you have rules in place for your e-mail? Do these rules include checking e-mail only a limited amount of times a day?
- Are you paperless? What have you done today to help your life become paperless?
- Do you have rules for your multitasking?
- Have you looked into hiring a coach?

STEP 6: CREATE ACCOUNTABILITY

If you hang out with chickens, you're going to cluck and if you hang out with eagles, you're going to fly.
—Steve Maraboli

THREE KEYS
1. Create a board of directors.
2. Have an accountability partner.
3. Review goals and accomplishments.

Grow Your Business...

Create a Board of Directors

Studies have shown that companies with a board of directors perform better over the long term than companies without a board. One of the main reasons for the better performance is that a board keeps the owner and employees accountable. In addition, your company may be required by state law to have a board of directors if your company is a corporation.

But how do you find the right people for your company? The first step is to interview prospective candidates in the community with skill sets that are useful and will bring value to your company. Don't sell yourself short. Go for well-established people who are successful or big players in your industry. Be prepared to compensate your board members either monetarily or with stock.

Board of Directors vs. Advisory Board

As a member of a board of directors, a board member has a legal obligation to shareholders and other stakeholders. The board member can be liable for company actions. As such, most board members are compensated, and the company usually keeps directors and officers on liability insurance. Advisory board members have no legal obligations and usually serve to help advise company management. The advisory meetings are usually less formal and usually cover requests for advice regarding complex business decisions. These boards are not mutually exclusive—companies can benefit from both boards at the same time.

Once you've created your board, use it to its full potential. Set up quarterly meetings and provide financial reports to the members. Work to maintain good relations with your board and actively draw from the collective experience of its members to help you with critical decisions.

Handbook Questions (for Your Company):

- Do you have a board of directors in place for your company? At a minimum, do you have an advisory board?
- Have you actively pursued board members?
- Do you hold regular board meetings?

Grow Your Life...

In your business you and your employees are accountable to fulfill job assignments. You have the same accountability for your life goals. Since there isn't a natural system of accountably in your life, you need to create the system from scratch. Here are ways to become accountable in your life.

Find an "Accountability Partner"

Find someone you can trust who is open to being a helpmate. This person can be a spouse, significant other, or co-worker. You can also have multiple partners, depending upon the stated goal. For example, you can tell your wife about your goal to take an exotic trip or start a charity but tell your trusted colleague about your goal to grow your company revenue by another 15 percent.

The important thing is to discuss your goals and the steps you are taking toward those goals. Set up times to discuss the steps you've taken or any revisions in the plan. If you know you must tell someone what you've accomplished, you're more likely to get moving.

Conduct Quarterly "Snapshots" & Annual Reviews

As already stated it's important to review your goals and accomplishments at least weekly. However, quarterly and annual reviews are just as important. Comparing your goals and bucket list items from one quarter and year to the next will give you a sense of the path you are taking, any gradual changes in perspective, and the trajectory of your journey.

For your quarterly snapshot, try writing down all of your life wins and accomplishments for the past quarter. These wins should tie back to your balance wheel. Here is an example:

- took trip with family
- added a big client at company
- joined tennis team
- got cholesterol down twenty points
- went to movie with Dad

Keep these quarterly snapshots in a place that you can refer back to. I keep mine in Evernote. I've heard life's accomplishments explained this way: "Self-growth is much like watching a child grow…day after day you do not see the improvement, whereas if you document the wins (similar to taking pictures of a child throughout the year) you will see much growth."

On an annual basis, make sure to review your goals for the year. Also be sure to rereview your bucket list and add to your bucket list once you start accomplishing much of the items on the list.

Handbook Questions (for Life):

- Do you have an accountability partner(s)?
- Have you discussed your goals and bucket list items with your accountability partner?
- Do you keep quarterly snapshots and annual reviews?

STEP 7: SPREADING THE WORD

You are what you share.
—Charles Leadbeater

> THREE KEYS
> 1. Incorporate social media into business.
> 2. Outsource your social media campaigns.
> 3. Don't let social media consume your personal life.

Grow Your Business...

S ocial Media

It's no secret that companies, large or small, need to be involved with social media. If you aren't on Facebook, Twitter, and LinkedIn, sign up now. If you've already entered the world of social media, you've probably discovered that being social is very time-consuming. For many companies with a staff that is already stretched too thin, developing an internal social media marketing team is just not feasible.

If this describes your predicament you may need to outsource these efforts to social media firms or consultants. This is certainly a sound strategy, but, the big question that looms for many is how much should I pay for social media marketing?

As a financial services executive who works with both small businesses and PR/marketing firms, here are my pricing insights.

Facebook, Twitter, LinkedIn
The Internet is swarming with companies ready to take on your social media needs. These companies will create accounts for your company and will also help in the running of synchronized promotional campaigns in various social media outlets. To get the full effect of social media,

postings need to be done at least once a day, but preferably more. Postings should not shout, "This is a promotion!" Instead, they should have some content value for your audience that perhaps points to your website for more information.

Unlike personal Facebook pages, business Facebook pages are discoverable through search engines. With a Facebook business page you can target your audience. A social media consultant will know what types of posts work best on Facebook and ways to entice people to like your page.

For Twitter, your chosen social media consultant should research hash (#) tags that are appropriate for your industry. Hash tags are similar to keywords in Google. They help people interested in particular subjects find the Twitter feeds they want to follow.

Companies specializing in social media will also research which LinkedIn groups are industry related and sign you up as a member. LinkedIn groups can open up new avenues for collaborations and clients. Groups also keep you up-to-date on industry news.

A comprehensive campaign that contains all of these elements could easily touch thousands of prospects on a daily basis. This is a very valuable service, and the range for a small company to invest in social media marketing should be somewhere between $5,000 and $7,000 per month.

Blog Development and Management

Many small companies are opting for the self-publishing method by bypassing the media filter and communicating directly with customers and prospects through a blog. You should be able to find a marketing partner or a social media consultancy that can handle all elements of a blog including content creation, podcasting, and social media dissemination through Twitter, Facebook, and other social media channels.

When hiring someone to write your blog, take a look at the blogs the person has written for other companies. Some firms "stuff" blogs with keywords so that the blog will be discovered in search engines, but these types of blogs tend to be unreadable. Also, Google is cracking down on "keyword stuffing" so you could be penalized for such behavior and drop in the Google rankings.

A company that has knowledge about your industry or takes the time to do the research, writes thoughtfully, and is more concerned about content than "stuffing" is the kind of social media partner you want for your company. The price range for this type of service for a small company should be somewhere between $5,000 and $10,000 per month (depending on the required blog activity).

Video

Creative campaigns that are tied into high-valued content such as video can be costly. However, not every online video has to appear as if Francis Ford Coppola produced it. By using the new mobile devices with great cameras, costs can be minimal. That said, more professional and creative videos cost about $10,000 per campaign.

Videos are being used more and more for marketing. Typically, videos on the web range between two and three minutes, just enough time to get your ideas across and for short-attention-span viewers to watch the whole video.

Posting videos on YouTube, which is another social media platform, can widen the viewing audience, as YouTube videos are discoverable in search engines and can easily be shared among friends and colleagues.

Handbook Questions (for Your Company):

- Have you gotten involved with social media for your business? Have you started a social media campaign?
- Have you outsourced your social media to a professional?
- Does your social media usage cover a wide range of avenues, including Facebook, Twitter, LinkedIn, a blog, and video?

Grow Your Life...

Whether you personally post or outsource, you probably use social media to promote your business. You should also establish a social media presence for your personal life. Unlike with your business, however, select only one social media vehicle so you do not spend (or waste) time updating various outlets.

Get Personal

Use your personal social media as another method of accountability. Connect with supportive friends and accountability partners. Post your goals and weekly steps you are taking to accomplish your dream and become an accountability partner for your friends.

Get Klout

Klout is a website that measures an individual's social influence. By analyzing the size of a user's social media network and the amount of social interaction, Klout assigns a number ranging from one to a hundred, which denotes how influential a person is—at least in the social media world. These numbers are used by companies and organizations trying to woo influencers to their products by giving perks. Perks can range from free stuff to airline and hotel upgrades. Although material benefits may not be one of your life's goals, it can't hurt you to get a perk now and then, especially if in the process of switching career gears your cash flow gets a little slow at times.

Handbook Questions (for Life):

- Have you used social media as a way to create accountability?
- Have you signed up for Klout? Do you know your Klout score?

CONCLUSION

Our greatest weakness lies in giving up. The most certain way to succeed is always to try just one more time.
—Thomas Edison

Scott Webster, who you met in the introduction and who had a profound impact on my life, took up motorcycle riding at a time most people would consider late in life. He was in his fifties, ready to sell his business to me and take on new life passions, and dying of cancer.

When he was diagnosed with inoperable cancer, he spent his time living life, making sure his family was provided for, and sharing his wisdom with his friends. Because of Scott, I continue to look for business opportunities with excitement and without negating the passion and goals of my life outside of work.

This book has been a memorial to Scott Webster, so I will leave you with the reassurance he gave me when I asked, "Can I grow a successful business and a fulfilling life?" His answer was a resounding "Yes, you can have both."

You too can have both!

ABOUT THE AUTHOR

Douglas Palmer, author of *A Practical Handbook to Starting a Successful Business*, is an accomplished entrepreneur and business advisor. For over two decades, he has been a CPA and CFO serving large and small organizations both domestically and abroad. He has personally started multiple companies and now advises business owners. His firm has been in business for over a decade and has been the sponsor of the University of Maryland entrepreneurial programs. Doug also works with students on a pro bono basis.

Doug serves on numerous boards and is the chairman of St. John's Community Services Foundation, one of the oldest charities in Washington, DC.

Doug, his wife, Deborah, and their three children live in Maryland just outside of Washington, DC.

www.ingramcontent.com/pod-product-compliance
Lightning Source LLC
Chambersburg PA
CBHW071804170526
45167CB00003B/1167